THE
GHOSTLY TALES
OF

DETROIT

Published by Arcadia Children's Books
A Division of Arcadia Publishing
Charleston, SC
www.arcadiapublishing.com

Spooky America is a trademark of Arcadia Publishing, Inc.

First published 2023

ISBN 978-1-4671-9741-0

Library of Congress Control Number: 2023937851

Notice: The information in this book is true and complete to the best of our knowledge. It is offered without guarantee on the part of the author or Arcadia Publishing. The author and Arcadia Publishing disclaim all liability in connection with the use of this book.

All images used courtesy of Shutterstock.com; p. 104 James Kirkikis/Shutterstock.com.

Spooky America

THE
GHOSTLY TALES
OF
DETROIT

DARALYNN WALKER

Adapted from Haunted Detroit by Nicole Beauchamp

arcadia
CHILDREN'S BOOKS

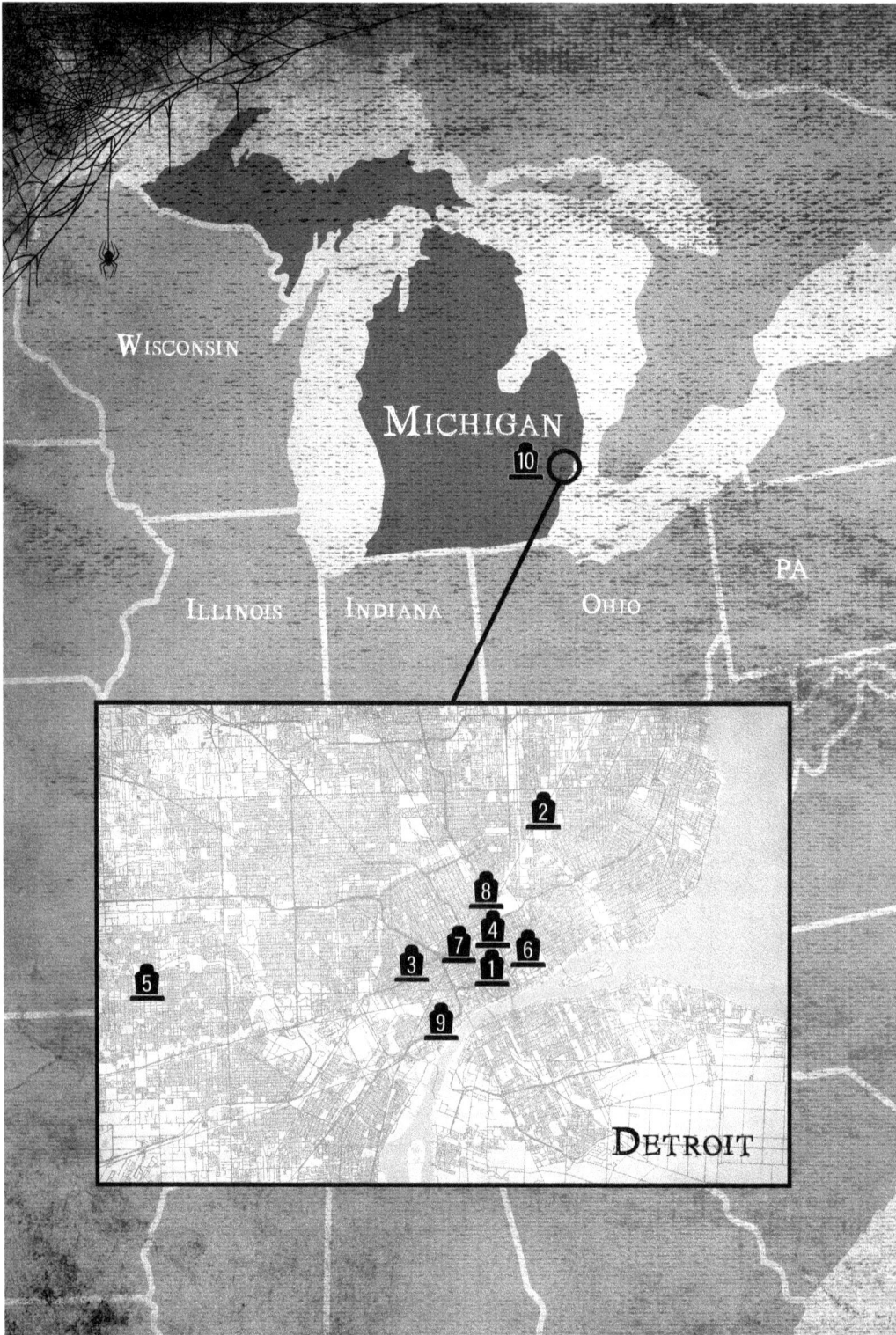

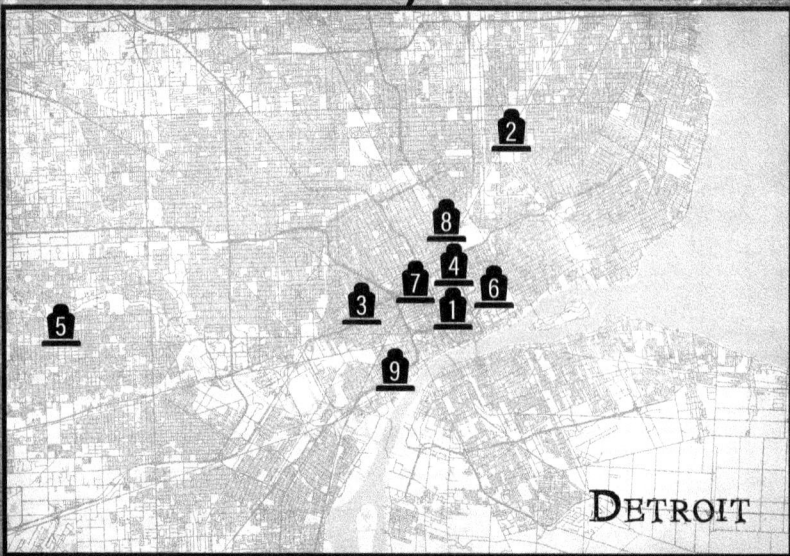

TABLE OF CONTENTS & MAP KEY

Welcome to Spooky Detroit!

When most people think of Detroit, they think of fast cars, Motown Records, and tasty food—and they would be correct! Often known as "Motown," "Hitsville USA," the "Motor City Capital of the World," or simply the "D," Detroit truly has it all: beauty, history, industry, music, art, and some pretty good pizza, too! Not to mention stellar snack brands like Vernors, Kar's Nuts, and Better Made Potato Chips—yum!

But did you know that Detroit also happens to be one of the most *haunted* cities in America? Yes, dear readers, lurking beneath all that music, food, history, and heritage, there's a whole spooky world just *waiting* to be discovered. A world full of creeps, crawlers, and phantasms galore roam Detroit's streets, watching and waiting for any unfortunate soul to fall straight into their fiendish hands!

But before we get into that ghastly business, you might be wondering: Where did all those ghosts come from? And how did Motor City become such a paranormal paradise? Well, maybe it's all the old battlefields in the area that date back hundreds of years. Maybe it's due to the great loss of life during the 1918 influenza pandemic. Or maybe, just *maybe*, it's got something to do with all those cars!

Back in the early twentieth century, Detroit had the distinct honor of being at the center of the automobile revolution. In fact, all three of the "Big 3" automakers—Ford, GM, and Chrysler—called Detroit home. Big car companies meant big opportunity, and people from all over the United States moved north in search of better jobs, better pay, and a better life for their families. Hundreds of thousands of people decided to make Detroit their home, and many decades later, engineers, car designers, and technicians are still clamoring for jobs with these automotive giants. What an impact!

In fact, some people who came to Detroit loved it so much, they have refused to leave— *even in death*! Today, ghosts are known to haunt all areas of the city. From old buildings and historic forts, to abandoned auto factories and creepy cafes—there is no shortage of spooky specters. And, really, it's no wonder so many spirits stick around. Just look at all the superstars who've called this great city home. In the 1940s and 50s, some of the most important musicians *ever* were getting their start in Detroit. Icons like Diana Ross and Aretha Franklin, who were part of an emerging record label based in Detroit (founded by a young entrepreneur named Berry Gordy) called Motown Records. Throughout the 1960s, Motown controlled the airwaves because so many hit songs—songs that you may still know today—were recorded in Detroit. Then, if we fast-forward a few decades, hip-hop innovator and international celebrity Eminem dominated the world's attention. Hailing from where, you might ask?

Nowhere other than Detroit, naturally!

And today, adoring fans stream hits from Big Sean and Lizzo, both having risen to fame from this musically rich city.

But Detroit is more than just a city with serious wheels, great eats, and a soul-spangled vibe. It holds an almost sacred place in history for being the last stop on the Underground Railroad, helping runaway slaves get to freedom. Sadly, many did not live to complete their journey, and some say those spirits still linger, their voices whispering along the riverfront.

So, don't let the razzle-dazzle of Detroit fool you. Under the veil of a majestic skyline and sparkling city lights that illuminate washed out, concrete-paved roads, there are plenty of secrets and legends about ghosts and frightening creatures sure to keep you awake all night!

Ready to explore ? Then, let's go!

The Hotel of Horrors

Rising twenty-two stories on the corner of Bagley Street and Cass Avenue in downtown Detroit quietly sits the Detroit Leland Hotel. Though it has obviously seen better days, this historic landmark has witnessed more than its fair share of murders, mobsters, and mayhem— and, of course, ghosts! With so many people passing in and out, phantoms of fright are often the main attraction at hotels. (Far more than the free breakfast and WIFI, anyway!) And at the Detroit Leland Hotel, ghostly guests are *always* welcome.

Built in 1927, the Leland was named after the automotive bigwig, Henry Martyn Leland. He was the founder of the Cadillac and Lincoln car companies. Now a dilapidated building and a shell of its former self, Detroit Leland Hotel was once considered a hidden gem of Detroit, with a beautifully decorated main lobby, eight hundred state-of-the-art guest rooms, a gorgeous ballroom, and more than a dozen stores. Guests marveled at the hotel's ornate staircase, brass chandeliers, big arched windows, and bustling bars and nightclubs. Detroit Leland Hotel was also a playground for partygoers, con artists, and excitable tourists to visit (or to make a quick buck!).

But though this picturesque

hotel was a sight to behold in its heyday, the same cannot be said for the Leland of today. In fact, some people think the hotel is undoubtedly haunted—maybe even cursed— due to the numerous murders, accidental deaths, and ghost sightings that have happened here.

(But we'll let *you* be the judge.)

The Detroit Leland Hotel was barely open for ten years before tales began to spread about the unexplainable deaths of hotel guests and visitors. As the years went on, the stories got more depressing and started to include tragic tales of fire and rough gangsters with their crooked activities. Over time, the hotel's reputation—and the building itself—fell into disrepair.

Currently, the Leland no longer operates as a hotel. Though a $120 million renovation was set to begin in 2018, the work never started.

The building remains open to this day and is home to a small number of residents and a longstanding nightclub, but the inside of the lobby emits a heaviness that is hard to explain. (To call it creepy would be an understatement!) Once bustling hallways are now dimly lit and eerily quiet. The walls are badly in need of paint and repair. Rows of stores now sit empty.

Except for the *ghosts*.

As it turns out, a deteriorating hotel is the PERFECT place to find ghostly guests—some of whom seem happy to stay for all eternity! Staff members, residents, and guests have all reported supernatural sightings. Can you imagine cleaning an empty room on an empty floor and suddenly hearing someone call your name? Well, that happened to a few housekeepers! Needless to say, they left and never came back. Some have felt the uninvited touch of hands grabbing them, while others have heard the melodic sounds of a piano playing with no pianist around! Talk about frightening!

Did we mention staying away from the fourth and seventh floors? After shutting down completely as a hotel, certain floors of the Leland were closed off due to terrible conditions, and among these floors were the fourth and seventh. It is said that the fourth floor has been swarming with paranormal activity for decades. Tenants would take the elevator up to that floor and couldn't access it, but they somehow still heard men walking around and talking. When they would report what they'd heard, they'd learn the floor was abandoned. The floor was said to be a hangout for Jimmy Hoffa, an American Labor Union leader, and his buddies. Mysteriously, Jimmy Hoffa disappeared in 1975 and has not been seen since. It is believed that his spirit still roams the Leland to this day. Talk about creepy!

The seventh floor, however, holds its own secrets. Upon heading to the forbidden floor, paranormal investigators felt a heavy presence when entering one of the rooms. The floor itself felt frozen in time, with lamps still illuminating the hallways and abandoned apartments still full of peoples' belongings— like they'd simply gone out for a walk and never returned. What a sight!

And if empty floors, mysterious piano players, and talking spirits don't get you stirred, just wait until we dig into some of the *really* bone-chilling tales of Detroit Leland Hotel. Are you ready to have your mind blown?

One summer, a young woman named Deandra went to visit her sister in Detroit. At the time, her sister was living at the Leland and wanted them to stay together, so Deandra happily obliged. She remembered walking into the building and having an eerie feeling but immediately shook it off. As the days went on, everything seemed normal, until one day she was awakened by the sound of choking in the middle of the night. The choking sounds continued for a few nights, and Deandra tried to ignore it, but after the third night, she knew she had to say something. She bolted into the hallway and politely asked the neighbor to keep it down. As soon as she spoke, the peculiar choking ceased, and she went back to bed.

The next day, Deandra told her sister about what happened, and a weird look came over her sister's face. Deandra explained how the last few nights were terrible: she had hardly gotten any sleep and was thankful the

neighbors decided to quiet down after she'd spoken to them. Her sister slowly grabbed her hand and took her outside of her apartment. When they stood in the hallway, Deandra's sister started opening the doors to the other apartments to reveal a whole floor of vacant rooms.

"I don't have any neighbors," Deandra's sister proclaimed.

Deandra just stared back in disbelief.

On her last night visiting, Deandra heard the choking sound again and decided to go and tell the front desk staff to check it out. But this time, she was in for a frightening surprise. As she came back up to the room, she suddenly heard a door slam loudly. Deandra whipped around to see a man in a suit eerily standing at the end of the hallway. As she fixed her eyes on him, she noticed his complexion was gray and that he had a hole in his neck! As he started to come toward her, she quickly ran into her sister's apartment and locked the door. The next morning, Deandra left the Leland and never returned.

Another married couple had a similar run-in with a ghost who wouldn't leave. One day, the husband came home from work to find a man sitting in one of the chairs of the living room. His wife was not home at the time, and he was completely puzzled. How had this man gotten into the house? He closed the front door behind him and sternly asked the gentleman, "How did you get in here?"

The intruder slowly nodded but didn't say anything.

In that same moment, the husband heard the sound of his wife turning the doorknob. He turned for a split second to call to her just as she

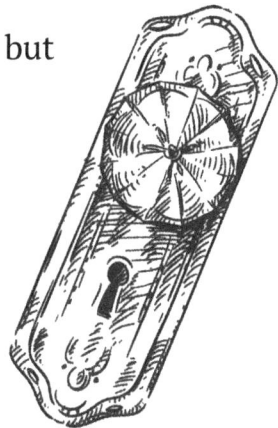

walked through the door with a basket full of laundry. He turned his attention once again to the stranger in his living room, but it was too late: the man had already vanished into thin air. Unfortunately, after a few more sightings that weren't quite as harmless and fleeting, the couple moved out with little more than

the clothes on their backs. I guess they weren't open to the idea of having roommates!

Speaking of stories, if the walls of the historic Detroit Leland Hotel could talk, what do you think they would say? Well, I guess the ghosts who now call it home could tell us. Would you dare enter a haunted hotel? I'm sure the souls hovering around would welcome you with open arms!

Beware
The Nain Rouge,
Detroit Devil
of Doom

When driving along the well-known Eight-Mile Road, made famous by the 2002 film *8 Mile,* starring rapper Eminem, no one ever stops to consider whether the stunningly historic buildings they pass have restless souls roaming around the dark corners and crevices of the building's corridors.

One of the oldest and most frightening legends that haunts Detroit is the Nain Rouge—a small, freakish devil that has appeared in countless Detroiters' nightmares since the inception of the city. It is described as a cursed demon that appears *right* before tragedy strikes. With razor-sharp teeth, glowing eyes, and a childlike frame, the Nain Rouge (which in French means "red dwarf") will give you goosebumps!

Its legend dates to 1701, when Antoine De la Mothe Cadillac, along with roughly one hundred fellow Frenchmen and another hundred Algonquian peoples, established Fort Pontchartrain du Détroit on a site that would eventually become downtown Detroit. Soon, Cadillac began having terrifying nightmares about a

"red imp" ruining his hopes and plans for the new city.

For years, he tried to brush off the bad dreams, but then one night, while taking an evening walk with his wife, his nightmare became a reality. Cadillac and his wife were strolling along a path when they saw a tiny but menacing figure appear suddenly, out of nowhere. As the tiny red troublemaker inched closer and closer, Cadillac and his wife froze in fear. They couldn't believe what they were seeing: his cold face, blazing eyes, and sinister grin were as clear as day, even in the moonlight.

Cadillac cried out as the Nain Rouge approached: "*Get out of my way!*"

But his demands were in vain.

The freakish creature burst into an evil laugh, then disappeared into the night.

From that point on, the downward spiral of Cadillac's life was set in motion and there was nothing Cadillac, nor anyone else, could do about it. Some say the Nain Rouge eventually drove him to madness.

Over the years, numerous people have reported encounters with the Detroit Devil of Doom, committing acts of sabotage and destruction, all the while promising more terror to come. Some say the story is just a tall tale, but every year, Detroit holds a parade to not only celebrate the city's history but also rid itself of the Devil of Doom. This so-called harbinger of evil is not welcome in Detroit, and each year, the city's residents, young and old, gather to make sure he is never seen or heard from again.

Many states in America have a variation of this story—such as the Devil of New Jersey—so if you're not so convinced, that's understandable. Maybe this story and others like it are simply that: stories. Little pieces of

American folklore that have passed through the ages and down to every generation.

But then...what *was* it that Antoine Cadillac and his wife stumbled upon on their walk that fateful night? What else could have driven him to near death, stuck inside a head tormented by madness?

Folklore can't explain that...at least not with any rhyme or reason accepted in this dimension.

Corruption, Case Files, and Creeps

As frightening as haunted hotels and cursed demons might be, trust us when we say they've got *nothing* on haunted prisons. Throughout history, prisons like Alcatraz in San Francisco, Eastern State Penitentiary in Philadelphia, and Ohio State Reformatory in Mansfield, were cavernous quarters concealing secrets so dark and *so* dangerous that prisoners often took them to the grave.

And even . . . *beyond.*

But what about a haunted police station?

Ed Steele Jr., owner and founder of the Historic Detroit 6th Precinct Restoration Project, purchased the old, dilapidated 6th precinct police building in 2013 for his cloud computing data center. Ed, a native Floridian who migrated to the north, had a vision to not only create an incredible IT space but also to build a community center and hire at-risk youth to work in the historic building. Incredible, right?

But as it turned out, the 26,274-square-foot limestone building had *visions* of its own . . .

Ed first stepped foot inside this massive former police station to start restoration efforts in 2014, and boy was he in for a surprise!

The conditions were so poor that he knew he was going to need to enlist reinforcements to get the building up to code. Trees were literally growing out of the bathrooms! The basement was flooded, and there were piles of old case files and mug shots laying around. Ed decided to have a garage sale to raise money for the restoration and pay for some urgent repairs. To assist with moving items from the building to where the garage sale would take place, he employed a five-person team. They had just finished a long day of hard, productive work when suddenly he heard what sounded like blood-curdling screams coming from the basement.

Instantly, Ed bolted down the steps to the basement as the other three men trailed

behind him to see what was going on. Once they reached the basement, they noticed the two female workers in a daze. "He touched my hair! He touched *me*!" one of the women repeatedly screamed, while the other shoved the phone in Ed's face. "I caught it on camera. Look!"

Puzzled and befuddled, Ed stood in silence as the five workers fled the scene, never to be seen again. Could it have been a ghost? Anything is possible, of course, when it comes to the paranormal.

What Ed didn't know was that in the early 1900s, the 6th precinct station unknowingly began its meteoric rise to fame as a paranormal hotspot. It was during this time that Detroit truly came into its own, as car factories sprung up along the banks of the Detroit River and the city's population and economy boomed. The population of Detroit increased from 285,705 in 1900 to 1.6 million in 1929. What a huge change!

In 1930, President Herbert Hoover allocated $1.8 billion toward developing new facilities that would create an abundance of construction jobs and assist with improving the country's infrastructure. Unfortunately, the United States was going through the Great Depression. People were losing jobs and businesses were closing all over the country, not to mention the fact that the automobile industry was declining in Detroit, despite the increase in population. Because Hoover had directed that the money should also pay for harbors, dams, highways, and public buildings, the city built a new police precinct, which soon became the 6th precinct.

As Ed started to do some research, the

pieces slowly came together as to why his team had run out on him. What he uncovered was alarming, to say the least.

Ed decided to do some digging on his own and contacted his friend Phil Conners, who speculated that the building might be haunted by ghosts. He immediately set up a meeting with two members of Detroit Paranormal Expeditions, Jeff and Todd, to conduct the first ever paranormal investigation at the precinct. This was going to be very interesting!

As soon as they began the tour, they went directly to the basement because, after all, that's where the staff members had first encountered the specter. It was a frigid winter's night, and the basement was icy cold. After walking around a bit, something strange happened: the men felt rocks pelting them. But the rocks weren't falling. They were being *thrown*.

And HARD.

Shaken, the men looked around but found nobody else. They were alone in the basement.

Weren't they?

A bit later, Todd moved into the evidence room to check it out. As he entered, he immediately felt a weird, uncomfortable energy surround him. All of a sudden, the door slammed loudly, trapping him inside the room with no way to escape! Todd called Jeff down to help him and, after a good amount of time working to pry the door open, a frightened Todd raced up the stairs as fast as he could. As they moved to other parts of the jail, they heard whistling coming from the cell block but couldn't find a source. The team used devices to capture voices inside the facility, and the responses that were heard would literally send chills up your spine.

Ed was particularly interested in learning

why so many paranormal teams kept gathering evidence there over time. He decided to visit the library to learn as much as he could about the building's history. As he researched, Ed could not unsee the graphic accounts and terrible tragedies that had occurred within the old precinct's walls. In newspaper clipping after newspaper clipping, he read stories and saw photos of gruesome killings, horrifying deaths, lethal gang activity, and heinous violent deeds—all at the precinct. No wonder

he and others felt such a heaviness—and such a dark energy—walking around inside the space.

Despite his findings, Ed was dedicated to restoring the precinct and working to build a better Detroit. Unfortunately, his vision would never come to pass. On August 25, 2021, Ed passed away at Beaumont Hospital at the age of 54.

Eerie Eats and Tasty Treats: Phantom Feasts at The Whitney

If you happen to be traveling through downtown Detroit, there are a few neighborhoods you must see. Many people love to visit our world-class theater district, which was built in the 1920s and is surrounded by the beautiful Grand Circus Park. In terms of the number of seats, the Detroit Theater District is the second biggest in the world. Only New York has a bigger theater area. How cool is that?

If you head north on Woodward, you'll reach our fantastic arenas, where you can catch performances by your favorite bands and watch your favorite teams play. Taking a stroll from the theater district to the arenas is a blast. You'll pass a lot of restaurants and historical sites, and you might even see a ghostly trolley floating down Woodward (make sure to wave!).

However, when you continue northward toward Midtown, it's hard to miss the majestic Whitney Mansion perched elegantly on the corner of Woodward Avenue. Built in 1894 for David Whitney Jr.'s beloved wife, Flora Whitney, this mansion has definitely seen its share of ghostly visitors! In fact, it's known for being one of the spookiest spots in all of Detroit. Once a beautiful family residence, the Whitney Mansion has been magically transformed into a restaurant and bar, and people from all over the world have come here to dine and socialize—with both the living *and* the dead!

What do you think? Are you ready to break bread with some ghosts?!

From very social specters that pull up a seat at the table beside you, to ghostly nurses that peer eerily out of windows, the historic Whitney Mansion houses the souls of many who have spent time here and decided they could never depart from its beautiful corridors.

Married in 1860 to David Whitney Jr.—the wealthiest man in Detroit—Flora gave birth to four children during their marriage: Grace, David III, Flora Ann, and Katherine. David Whitney was a hardworking man and in his heart wished only to make Flora happy. So, when she said she wanted to build a home "befitting of his status," David immediately started planning the most extravagant mansion Detroit had ever seen! Construction began in 1890 and took four years. That might sound like a long time to build a house, but considering it was the first home in Detroit to have a personal elevator, it makes sense the mansion took so long to build. David saw to it that the mansion truly had the best of everything! Totaling 21,000 square feet—with 42 rooms, 10 bathrooms, and 20 fireplaces—David Whitney paid $400,000 to have it built, which would be over $10 million in today's money! (And that's not even counting the money he had to spend to decorate it!)

But money, of course, can't buy love. And in life, sadly, nothing is guaranteed. David unfortunately learned this lesson for himself. On February 7, 1882—eight years before construction on the mansion even began—David received the devastating news that his dear wife had passed away. She would never live to see David's grand vision come to life.

Nonetheless, David kept his promise. He moved forward with building the home in Flora's honor and, once it was complete, the family moved right in. Whitney's family remained at the estate until 1920, long after the elder David's death in 1900. Today, Flora's soul is said to still linger in the Whitney estate, despite the fact that she was never able to reside there.

Perhaps she is unaware she is dead and trying to locate her husband or family. Or maybe she has simply come to admire the mansion that David built in her honor. We may never know how Flora came to haunt a place she never came to know in life, but some people claim to have encountered her sobbing uncontrollably in certain rooms of

the house. Her cries are said to be filled with a profound anguish that can be felt by anyone who hears them.

One diner, in particular, claims she noticed Flora on the third floor lounge near the ladies' restroom. The young lady was having a nice evening out with friends and headed to the bathroom to freshen up. Just as she was about to enter, she noticed a woman dressed in outdated clothing crying loudly on the couch.

"Excuse me, miss. Are you all right?" she asked.

The crying woman didn't respond. Instead, she started to cry even louder! The young woman was so disturbed by how sad the woman seemed, she quickly left the lounge to find the manager and report the incident. But by the time they came to check in on the woman, she had vanished! They even checked the security footage, and she was nowhere to be found. Talk about scary!

Another patron who visited the restaurant on a slow weekday paid a visit to the same lounge and, boy, was she in for a shock!

The bartender had just finished making her a drink and sat it down where the young lady was sitting. But after an hour of her being gone, he realized that she had not returned from the restroom. Finally, when the woman returned, the bartender approached her and asked if everything was okay.

"Oh, I was just having a conversation with your bathroom attendant," the woman replied.

"Bathroom attendant?" The bartender blinked. "I'm sorry, ma'am, we don't have bathroom attendants here."

Soon, the woman began describing the attendant from head to toe to prove she was telling the truth, but the bartender told her repeatedly the person she was talking with didn't exist.

"Well, I know who I was talking to," the lady insisted.

After much back and forth (and feeling a little irritated), the young lady dragged the bartender to the restroom to prove to him he was wrong. Much to her dismay, however, no one was there. After chatting with management and reviewing security tapes, the bartender was proven right. Nobody matching the woman's description had entered or exited the building.

To this day, the case of the mysterious bathroom attendant remains unsolved.

The staff of the Whitney Mansion are well aware of all the claims of spooky activity. One night, the restaurant's general manager had an experience that scared him so much, he says he'll never step foot in the mansion alone again. It was late, and everyone else had already left for the night. Before heading home, the general manager began taking his usual walk through the mansion, checking that everything was locked up and secure. He had nearly finished his rounds, when suddenly, he heard the faint, melodious sounds of a piano playing somewhere in the distance. In that instant, a heaviness settled over him that he just couldn't shake. He knew he needed to investigate.

One by one, as the eerie sound of music drifted through the halls, he began checking all the rooms with pianos. But each time, he came up empty. Every piano sat silent and untouched. And yet . . . the music played on.

Finally, there was only one room left to check. The general manager cautiously headed down to the first floor. With every step, he felt his apprehension—and the heaviness in his chest—intensify. When at last he reached the ground floor piano, the music suddenly halted. The chilly silence that followed scared him so much, he bolted like a spooked horse.

After the passing of his beloved Flora, David Whitney ultimately remarried, and his new wife (who happened to be Flora's sister) was apparently very particular about making sure all household items were kept in the right place. These days, The Whitney's basement is a storage facility for dishes, pots, pans, and other supplies for the entire restaurant. But can you guess what *else* you might find in the basement?

You guessed it: a ghost!

The staff have repeatedly claimed that going down there can get pretty crazy. Sometimes it's hard to find items because they get moved all around. There have been a lot of claims of items going missing and ending up on other floors. It seems as though the second Mrs. Whitney is hard to appease when it comes to cleanliness. Talk about being a perfectionist to the very end!

Even crazier than the basement, however, is the Whitney Mansion's infamous elevator.

You may have heard of the Tower of Terror at Disney and the crazy ride the elevator inside takes you on—but *nothing* compares to the creeptastic horrors that lie in wait in the elevator of the Whitney Mansion. One Thanksgiving, a family decided to have dinner

at The Whitney. In hopes of avoiding the walk up the stairs, they decide to take the elevator. The father pushed the button, not thinking anything of it. But as soon as the doors opened, the little boy's eyes went wide in horror. To his surprise, the elevator was *full* of decrepit, human-like individuals in old clothing from a different time.

The child immediately recoiled with a shudder. "I can't go in!" he exclaimed.

"Why can't you?" his parents asked inquisitively.

The boy shook his head. "There is no room for us."

A little perplexed, his parents hurriedly dismissed his claims, scooped him up, and carried him into the elevator without another thought. This, among other stories of the elevator operating by itself, have plagued The Whitney since the early 1900s.

Want to hear something else creepy? Behind the Whitney Mansion, David Whitney built a carriage house (a historic building that at one time held horses and carriages). The oldest daughter, Grace, used the carriage house as her own private place of rest, and it is believed her spirit never left. Throughout the years, Grace enjoyed viewing polo tournaments from the carriage house window while sipping a cup of tea.

After she died in 1938, the family hired a company to pack up Grace's things. Just as the movers started to carefully pack Grace's old tea set, the carriage house filled with the sounds of doors slamming, papers flying messily off desks, and women's heels hitting the floorboard. It was clear to the movers that someone—or some*thing*—was not happy with them for touching the tea set. Fear gripped the team so badly, they decided to put it right back where they'd found it. Even today, the tea set remains undisturbed!

A frightening nurse's specter appears to be another of the hostile spirits known to appear in the carriage house. Before it became a restaurant, The Whitney was a hospice (or home for the sick) for people with tuberculosis. Many nurses have been in and out of the residence, both as employees and patients. People have seen an evil-looking woman with hollowed-out eyes looking out of a window in the carriage house, watching people come and go from the valet parking lot. No one knows her story or how she came to haunt the carriage house, but those who have seen her have been horrified by her sinister, ghostly face.

Even though the Whitney Mansion wasn't a private home for very long, it certainly seems to be a "forever home" to plenty of ghosts! What do you think? Are you brave enough to spend a day (or even a night) exploring a real-life haunted mansion? Would you stop to say hello to a ghostly bathroom attendant, or sip a spooky cup of tea? Would you ride a ghostly elevator, or wave to the otherworldly woman in the carriage house window?

Or ... would you *run*?

A visit to The Whitney will uncover a rich and beautiful history of the City of Detroit. But should you choose to visit this lavish dwelling—complete with hidden passageways, sprawling gardens, delicious American cuisine, and maybe even a piano-playing ghost—one thing is for certain: *enter at your own risk.*

Descent into Madness

It's hard to believe that just a short car ride from the elegance and charm of the Whitney Mansion sits a site so spooky and *so* notoriously haunted, it could easily be out of a horror movie. Indeed, one of Michigan's most infamous asylums is located a mere sixteen miles west of the city's energetic downtown. Westland, Michigan, is a Detroit suburb long known for the Eloise Asylum. Opened in 1839 as a home for Michiganders in desperate need, it quickly grew to become one of the largest public healthcare facilities in the United States.

In those days, patients suffering from mental health issues were often treated roughly, even inhumanely, and Eloise Asylum ultimately became notorious for the atrocities it committed on its patients. Today, few structures remain from the original hospital of horrors, located on a vast 160 acres of land, but legend has it that countless wandering souls still call this place home.

Sadly, the tragedy of Eloise Asylum is not only that it existed at all, but also that it was one of many similar facilities across the United States at that time. One major problem was that science, and our understanding of mental illness, was simply not like it is today. Scientists often performed surgeries and procedures that did far more harm than good, if any good at all.

If that wasn't bad enough, people sometimes brought their family members to places like Eloise Asylum to live out the rest of their lives, dropped like newspapers at the front door.

Can you imagine doing that to any of your loved ones? The idea is virtually unthinkable!

Nonetheless, many of Detroit's elderly, disabled, and less fortunate were handed off to the open arms of evil! Even babies and orphans were sent to Eloise, forced to live alongside people with genuine mental health issues—poor souls who never received the individual care they needed. It was a tragic and unfortunate time in history for science and humanity.

From 1839 to 1881, doctors from Detroit and Wayne would visit the hospital once or twice a week, but it wasn't enough. There were simply too many people, and they couldn't keep track of how patients were doing. In 1868, the city decided to build an official asylum specifically for persons with mental illness, but it was not a treatment facility to say the least. There was no resident doctor on site and individuals would be chained to walls or even locked in darkened rooms to supposedly help them calm down. Lobotomies (procedures involving the removal of, or altercation to, different parts of the brain) were performed on patients, as well as electroshock therapy, a form of "treatment" that involves shocking a person's brain with an electric current.

Terrifying, right?

In 1881, though, Eloise Asylum was in store

for some BIG changes. The supervisory staff made it a rule that caretakers had to have a medical degree, and Dr. E.O. Bennett was the first doctor to be the property's keeper. People said that he really cared about the patients and stopped a lot of the cruel things being done to them. Many individuals thought that his experiments had helped many people get better. A victory for the science world!

By the early 1900s, the Eloise community had its own chapel, bakery, laundry services, railroad stop, and other things people needed to live. Some of the staff even moved into affordable housing alongside the patients they cared for. They started to grow families of their own. Things were looking up, or so they thought . . .

In 1931, one of the buildings on the same property was reconstructed into a general hospital open to the public. But as the United States faced the Great Depression (a period of history when America's economy failed and many people lost their homes), the new hospital quickly became packed with over two thousand poverty-stricken individuals. Leadership tried to keep up with the growth, but unfortunately, it was not successful. By 1933, 7,441 people were occupying the site, while an additional 2,600 people were added to the already crowded psychiatric wards at Eloise. To illustrate how bad it was, over one hundred women had to share a handful of toilets. Things were taking a turn for the worse, again.

Patients' living conditions were filthy, and employees were overworked. It got to the point where orderlies were giving patients unnecessary treatments just to keep them calm. The 1940s were dark days for Eloise, as the severity of treatment was getting worse. Patients were put through brutal procedures such as being chained to tables, restrained in straitjackets, and forced to take baths in either freezing cold or scorching hot water. Suffice it to say, this torture tragically caused many fatal accidents to befall patients.

Then, a breakthrough happened in 1977. The state stopped funding the asylum, and on December 1, 1979, Eloise closed its doors after almost 150 years in operation. Now, the only thing that remains are scattered structures, horrific memories, and the Eloise cemetery, where seven thousand patients were laid to rest with nothing more than a numbered marker to identify them.

Considering the site's brutal and disturbing history, it's no surprise at all that the land where Eloise Asylum once stood is among the most haunted locations in America.

Paranormal explorers have ventured through the remaining buildings, and what they have found over the years would surely knock your socks off! From disheveled elderly spirits roaming the outside of the property, to the sound of children playing in a now vacant playground, the heaviness of the atmosphere alone will send chills up and down your spine. The historic Kay Beard building is the only building the public has access to. It has become a popular local attraction for haunted history tours, paranormal investigations, and to host haunted houses.

People from all over the world have traveled to Detroit to explore this now vacant property. This asylum harbors secrets of torture, cruelty, neglect, and sheer wickedness that may very well still keep thousands of tormented souls in a state of anguish. Their secrets can be heard in whispers as you walk the grounds. In the swishing of curtains and shoving of doors.

If you ever dare to visit, remember to explore with caution. Some of these patients were known to be violent in their previous lives. And in death . . . you never know how angry their souls might still be.

Behind the Veil

When you think of cemeteries, what usually comes to mind? You might picture creepy headstones and eerie iron gates. You might think of full moons and dark, sinister shadows. You might think of the walking dead, of ghoulish ghosts, of skeletal fingers reaching up through the ground to grab you by the—

Ahhh!

Phew, you got away. (But just barely.)

The good news is, Detroit's historic Elmwood Cemetery is unlike any other cemetery you've probably ever seen or imagined! With rolling green hills and a creek running through it, this picturesque eighty-six-acre property is sure to impress even the most apprehensive guests. This historically rich estate serves as the final resting place for some of Detroit's finest: mayors, ministers, lawyers, doctors, and dignitaries are buried and memorialized here, as well as famous abolitionists (people who fought for slaves to be free), and many soldiers and war heroes—men and women who fought for the freedoms Americans enjoy today.

Some visitors, however, have reported seeing a lot more than just tributes. After all, with all that history, there's almost *guaranteed* to be some ghosts hanging around. Apparitions of soldiers in red coats have been said to appear, some severely injured or in distress.

While no British soldiers are buried here (that we know of), random sightings of ghosts dating back to the American Revolutionary War have happened over the years, with some claiming to have seen wispy figures wandering among the graves.

(How spooky is that?!)

Long before this cemetery even *became* a cemetery, this land belonged to the area's Indigenous peoples, who zealously guarded it. Through countless wars and invasions—and many lives lost—they were aware of the tranquility and peace that this land possessed.

Among the beautifully landscaped gardens and certified arboretum stands a twelve-foot-tall marble sculpture of a floating woman with a veil delicately draped over her face. The sculpture originally came from Rome and was lost for several years following a shipwreck near Spain! It took close to two years for people to find and recover the statue—but guess what happened next! On the statue's second voyage—this time traveling up the Hudson River—it fell off the ship *again*! By the time the sculpture finally made it to Elmwood Cemetery, it had been through quite a journey. (Would you believe that during a bad storm in 1919, the statue fell over and was damaged a THIRD time?) No wonder people say that anyone who dares to gaze at the veiled woman will be destined for eternal ruin and damnation.

But we'll let you be the judge!

The monument was erected for Eliza Davenport, wife of Joshua Whitney Waterman. They were married on July 4, 1846, in the state of New York. They relocated to Detroit and had four children: three sons and a daughter. All was going well for the young couple until Eliza passed away suddenly in 1865. The grieving husband designed this memorial in Eliza's honor. The statue was sculpted and shipped from Rome, but following the shipwreck, it took years to get to the United States! (Can you imagine waiting *years* for your package to arrive? Where's Amazon Prime when you need it?!) But nonetheless, the beautiful monument was such a work of art, it was obviously worth the wait.

If you're brave enough to visit Elmwood Cemetery and pay tribute to the veiled woman, be alert. You just may find the spirit of Eliza Davenport sitting in the backseat of your car.

Terror on Woodward Avenue

I'm sure you've heard the oh-so-spooky tales of haunted libraries across the United States, where visitors claim to have witnessed all *kinds* of abnormal activity, including ghostly librarians floating by, mysterious footsteps, and frightening sounds that are so strange and mysterious, they'll give you the heebie-jeebies.

But what if I told you that the ghostly sightings that happen at the main branch of the Detroit Public Library will send chills down your spine? This grand historic landmark has been perched at the corner of Woodward and Warren since 1865, drawing the attention of community organizations, schools, and celebrities alike. The iconic entrance alone is sometimes compared to the grand entryways of a European palace!

The Main Library was designed to be a place of learning and study, and as Detroit's population increased in the 1950s, so did the library. With its vibrant flowing colors and local flair, the art and murals in the library transport you as you wander its open, airy corridors. One of the neatest things about the main branch is that it holds the Burton Historical Collection, which has super cool historic maps, land records, and interesting facts about former generations. Locals and book lovers know it as a treasure trove.

Can you picture yourself working alone in this beautiful building? Hearing the squeaky, creaky doors open and close, or exploring the dim, winding corridors that house what seems like hundreds of books? What would you do if you heard voices or, better yet, footsteps coming from a distance when no one else was around? Although the staff tends to stay silent about the library's paranormal activity (after all, they don't want to frighten off visitors), one brave soul opted to speak her mind.

A former Detroit Public Library employee by the name of Alejandra Amalia worked within

the Burton collection for two and a half years. She spent a large part of her day gathering documents and items for visitors doing research. This 140,000-square-foot library has multiple floors, and while a large part of the Burton collection is held on the upper floor under lock and key, a good portion is also held in the gloomy, dark, shadowy sub-basement in a climate-controlled vault. Talk about creepy!

The aisles of this sub-basement were so dim that Alejandra described it as being "so dark down there that you could barely see your hand in front of your face." Because it was part of the job, the employees dealt with it, but no one wanted to go down into the eerie cellar.

Imagine this: You're in the basement to retrieve documents, trying your best to ignore the voice in your head telling you to *run*. With no cell phone service, hardly any light, and air so silent and unsettling, you can hear a pin drop, your stomach is in your throat. The sooner you can get out of there, the better!

One day Alejandra's supervisor tasked her with organizing some files in the basement vault. As she proceeded down each row, Alejandra flicked on every bookcase lamp to break the darkness. She took a deep breath and reminded herself there was nothing to be afraid of. This was just like any other library room. Books. Papers. Shelves. No big deal, right?

Wrong.

As she got into her work, a frightening feeling suddenly came over her. Alejandra had an unsettling sensation that someone— or some*thing*—was down in the basement with her. This easy task was becoming more complicated by the minute!

Alejandra pushed past her feelings and continued on, but as she returned to organizing the files and photos, she heard a sound that stopped her in her tracks. It was a faint noise that broke the vault's deafening silence.

At this point, Alejandra could not focus, and she had to find out where this clatter was coming from. The sound of small feet pitter-pattering across the room filled her with anxiety and dread, but she had to check it out. As she peered around the bookcases into the darkness of the vault, her heart raced! Something was there with her, but who? Or *what?* Was it a mouse? Could another person have snuck downstairs without her noticing? Possibly. But why? Why make one very scary place even scarier?!

After a few minutes of silence, Alejandra decided to shake the feeling off, but the

noise came back with a vengeance! This time, Alejandra edged out farther to see if she could see anything at all, but again, she found nothing. She was becoming more annoyed than scared. She decided to focus even harder on her work and just get the job done so she could get out of there as quickly as possible.

But as the saying goes, third time's the charm, and the noise suddenly seemed *much* closer as Alejandra gazed down the dimly lit aisle. Then, out of nowhere, came a flash of movement. She caught sight of something about three feet tall zipping past the bookshelves. Alejandra immediately froze in shock. Her hands became clammy, and her heart felt like it was going to implode. A moment later, to her horror, the tiny blur ran past her *again*, this time heading in a different direction. She couldn't believe what she was seeing: the terrifying figure appeared to be a gnome wearing a red pointed cap and clothing. Alejandra didn't know what to do, and after a few moments of standing paralyzed in shock, she raced for the first exit she could find, abandoning everything, including her work.

To this day, Alejandra believes it was the Nain Rouge, and although she never

encountered the devilish creature again, current staff members avoid the vault at all costs. Some say the historic documents held within the Burton Historical Collection have supernatural attachments and strange energies. Even the bravest souls are wise enough to stay as far away from the vault as humanly possible!

Sit Back, Here Comes the Axe

Cults, curses, and headless men walking around Detroit. Can you believe that? Does it sound interesting?

Well, what else would you expect in this awesomely spooky city?

In 1904, an Italian immigrant named Benjamino Evangelista, migrated to Detroit for a better life. After making some money in real estate, "Benny"—who considered himself a mystic and a healer—began selling medicinal herbs and "black magic" to vulnerable people looking for help in all the wrong places. He even went so far as to create his own "bible" and preached his religious beliefs to anyone who would listen. As fate would have it, people started to follow Benny's teachings, and he eventually founded a cult. (A cult is a group of people with a religion or set of beliefs that many regard as extreme or even dangerous.)

Benny truly believed that God was sending him visions, and that he should share those visions with others. He referred to himself as a "Divine Prophet" and wore a wig and beard to make himself appear wiser than he was. Before long, Benny started to gain the reputation of Detroit's "Hex Man."

That's quite a name!

Benny met and married a woman named Santina, and the two parented four children together. Thanks to his success in real estate and carpentry, he was able to provide a good life for his family and move them to a beautiful neighborhood on St. Aubin and Mack. Sounds like the American Dream, right?

In the new home, Benny dedicated his basement to his black magic. It was an escape from the day to day, and though some considered him a religious extremist, others followed him blindly, bought his herbs, attended his church meetings, and even read his bible. With Benny's growing fame, however, came an increasing number of critics and accusers. They believed he was a scam artist taking advantage of desperate people who really needed help. Benny's popularity diminished as people started to realize his cures weren't working. Plain and simple, they saw him for what he was: a con man.

Benny was well aware of what people

thought of him and his unorthodox practices. However, he wouldn't know how serious they were about destroying him until the evening of July 3.

On the night of July 3, 1929, Benny was working on his carpentry business when he contacted a watchman to deliver lumber to his home that evening. Well, the next morning, there was no lumber, no delivery man, and Benny was found to have been *beheaded* in his home with an axe!

To this day, many say the land where Benny once lived is haunted. There have been reports of disembodied (so to speak) voices in

the middle of the night coming from out of nowhere, and reports of headless men roaming around the neighborhood. Even though the case was never solved, and Benny's home was demolished years ago, people still know his case as one of the most unusual in Detroit's history.

If you're a true daredevil, venture down St. Aubin Street to see the desolate land where "Benny Evangelist's" home once stood.

But make sure you keep your distance ... unless you *want* a close encounter with a headless man.

CHAPTER 9

Soldiers of the Shadows

Isn't it peculiar that just ninety-six acres of land can hold stories of the living *and* the dead for centuries? Well, visitors from all over the world flock to Old Fort Wayne to experience the strange sights and eerie apparitions that have been quietly residing there since 1701, when Cadillac and his band of French explorers first arrived. Have you ever heard the expression, "*If these walls could talk?*" Well, according to many spooktacular legends, the Fort Wayne barracks, which at one time included an officers' quarters, hospital, recreation building, and a guard house, has had more than its fair share of walls talking, screaming, yelling, and even keeping watch over this historic site. (Don't forget, this is also where Cadillac and his wife first spotted the Nain Rouge!)

Built in the early 1840s to protect American soldiers from possible British attack after the war of 1812, Fort Wayne was never a battleground, though many deaths occurred there over the centuries. From a large-scale flu pandemic to accidental casualties, this land holds many secrets, tragedies, and shocking truths.

Let's learn more about this frightening fort, shall we?

For thousands of years, Indigenous peoples used the area where Fort Wayne now stands as burial mounds. Over time, thanks to theft, erosion, farming, and, eventually, building construction, nearly all the mounds were destroyed. The fort itself took eight years to build and is located alongside the Detroit River, less than a half mile from the Canadian shore. (Did you know that Michigan and Canada are neighbors?) This new garrison (a fort, in military terms) was named Fort Wayne after Anthony Wayne, an important officer in the American Revolutionary War.

As with many military forts, a pair of large, leaden doors guarded the entrance. Unfortunately for some of the soldiers standing guard, some of the mistakes made were deadly! The first soldier known to have died tragically was a young man by the name of William Pickett. As other soldiers moved cannons and loaded them into embrasures (pretty much a place to hold the cannons), William Pickett stood guard in front of the massive doors at the fort's entrance. Weary from the day's work, several soldiers mistakenly let a cannon escape their grasp. But before they could do anything to stop it, the cannon hurled violently toward the front doors and right for Soldier Pickett. The cannon struck William, and he died instantly, thus becoming Fort Wayne's first known casualty... and possible first known ghost?

Visitors to the fort have reported seeing an armed soldier stationed at the entrance. Perhaps that's Soldier Pickett himself, still on duty and protecting the fort, even in death? Next time you're in Detroit, make sure to stop by and say hello. After all, you never know... maybe he'll say hello right back!

Many have speculated about the

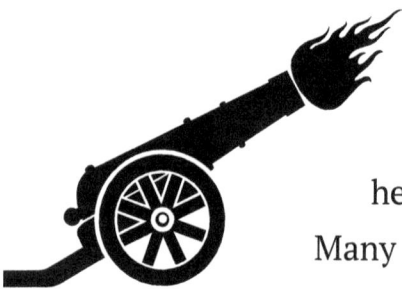

accuracy of the legends surrounding the Fort Wayne grounds, but only Ed Kachadoorian has the inside scoop. Not only has Ed worked as a tour guide and paranormal investigator for Haunt Investigators of Michigan, he has spent years studying the paranormal in the Detroit area, making him a certified expert on the subject.

Ed and others claim that the fort is also haunted by the souls of former slaves, as Detroit was the final stop on the Underground Railroad. To test this theory, Ed and a team of ghost hunters started doing some investigative research. The team collectively visited the old fort grounds and decided to use an ITC device (ITC stands for Instrumental Trans Communication), a machine that basically turns readings from the surroundings into spoken words, and what they uncovered was hair-raising!

As they sat in darkness, Ed started to ask questions out loud. Almost right away, he got answers. A spirit was talking to him! They quickly learned the spirit's name was Isaac Cook, a former slave whose wife had been sold away. Isaac had tried many times to find his beloved wife, but after failing to locate her, he decided to escape by swimming across the Detroit River to Windsor, Ontario. Unfortunately, Isaac did not survive the swim. He drowned before he could reach the Canadian shoreline to claim his freedom. Despite its tragic conclusion, this historic account ranks among the most out-of-this-world paranormal encounters of all time for Ed. He said it was the first and last time ever in his career that a ghost had told him his first AND last name. Pretty spooky stuff!

Without a doubt, the old fort grounds are most definitely haunted with soldiers in the shadows. One story in particular stands out as quite humorous. A male member of the Historic Fort Wayne Coalition had an unforgettable experience with a Civil War soldier. While volunteering one day, he was inspecting the grounds of the property and felt a strong grip on his backside! (p.s. That means his butt!) When he turned around, no one could be found, but for the rest of the day, the volunteer found himself being groped by invisible hands, and he had a strange sense that someone was following him. Sounds like someone had a spooky secret admirer!

Have you ever felt a chill race down your spine or heard a bump in the night and thought it was a ghost? Most of the time, we just ignore it, but at Fort Wayne, what goes bump in the night may very well be a "spirited" visitor!

One chilly fall evening, two ghost hunters were stationed on the first floor of the recreation hall. They were talking about the legend of a soldier who was a bully, both in life and death. Little did they know, he also happened to be occupying the room they were standing in! The first ghost hunter turned out the lights and the room went pitch black. Immediately, the second ghost hunter, Jenny, felt a menacing presence enter the space. Then, she heard footsteps approaching! Unwilling to back down, she stood firm, even as a frightening figure came barreling toward her. In one fell swoop, Jenny felt the presence of the being quickly come and go, with only a bitter chill left in the room. As her partner ran

to her side, Jenny realized what had happened. This ghost was a belligerent soul who enjoyed pushing people around. But Jenny had been brave and strong, and the ghost never bothered her again. Looks like it messed with the wrong woman!

Another close encounter happened when a ghost hunter named Rick decided to investigate the officers' quarters on his own. He was pretty brave, too! Fortunately for him, a less experienced investigator showed up to study Rick's techniques. I'm sure she never thought she'd witness what they were about to see!

As they were walking the fort's long hallways, Rick yelled into each doorway they passed to see if any spirits were inside. After no luck, he decided the ghosts might not be in the mood to communicate. But when they finally reached the last door, it began to close slowly—*all on its own*. Thinking it was another investigator playing a trick on him, Rick yelled out, "Yeah, whatev—" but mid-sentence, the door suddenly slammed inches from his face, then bounced off the door jamb and opened completely! Shocked and amazed, the two peered inside, but the room was empty. What a rush! Deep down, even though they couldn't see anyone, something told Rick they were definitely *not* alone. They even have video footage to prove it.

Not only has the Old Fort Wayne been a national attraction for paranormal tours and television shows, it also now serves as a community venue that hosts festivals, weddings, meetings, and other local events. The ghostly inhabitants here aren't going anywhere, so when you get a chance, stop by, take some pictures, and enjoy all the history the grounds have to offer.

And who knows?

Maybe you'll even meet some ghostly companions that can show you around.

Illusions of Evil

Have you ever dreamed of owning your very own haunted house? Well, the Terebus brothers (Jim and Ed) turned that dream into a reality. Not only have they been in the haunted house business for forty-two years and counting, they founded Erebus Haunted Attractions, one of the nation's top haunts! They settled on the name "Erebus" after Ed came across the word in a vampire book. "Erebus" felt both creepy and fun, plus it was very close to their last name, Terebus—and so Erebus Haunted Attractions was born.

In 1998, the brothers bought an enormous one-hundred-thousand-square-foot building to house their haunted attraction. Imagine their surprise when they discovered that their "haunted house" really was haunted! Since the first day they set foot on the property, which had been empty for forty years before they bought it, they have been plagued with paranormal experiences.

Ed, who briefly lived in the building during the beginning of construction, couldn't shake the feeling that he wasn't alone late at night, even though he couldn't explain it. He'd hear all kinds of strange noises, like footsteps, clanking, banging, and on one occasion, a raspy voice calling his name over and over through a wall—so much for a getting a good night's sleep!

On multiple occasions, Ed was so convinced someone had broken in that he even called the police, but they never found another soul. (At least ... not another *living* soul.) Some of the neighbors told them that many years earlier, a homeless man who had been living in the building's basement froze to death.

Could *he* be the spirit keeping Ed up all night?

Even the employees have had curious, paranormal seeming experiences within the building. They've seen shadowy figures walking through walls, heard doors being slammed loudly, and even found random scratches on their own bodies they couldn't explain. They have been locked behind random doors, observed floating orbs inside their cars, and—scariest of all—witnessed *disembodied heads* floating from the ground and huge disfigured masses running toward them. Once, after an extremely spine-tingling encounter, the Erebus art director, Steve, saw a "looming shadow person" in a photo he'd taken—from the room he'd just been in!

Even though Ed and Jim did not plan on their haunted house *actually* being haunted, it has definitely brought the employees closer and kept them on their toes!

One of the employees said, "I do not scare easily, but every day when I get to work, I go straight into my office and pray out loud. This is the only place where I can look into the darkness and feel it looking back at me."

But even with all the unusual happenings, most employees seem to enjoy working at Erebus. Not only are they dedicated to giving guests a *ghoulishly* good time, they enjoy putting on a show for the crowds. It's no wonder Erebus attracts worldwide attention and draws people from all over the country. In 2005, the haunt was the first of its kind to make the Guinness Book of World Records for the world's longest walk-through haunted attraction. What an accomplishment!

In 2019, *USA Today* readers ranked Erebus the number one haunted attraction in the country. They have been featured on television shows around the world, and every year throw one of the best, scariest Halloween shows *anywhere*.

Just like their ghostly friends, the production only seems to get better with time.

After all, it's probably the only place you will find in the metro Detroit region where men, women, and children will pay to go year after year to be scared.

Be sure to visit Erebus as Halloween draws near to get in the spirit of the holiday. This is *the* place to go if you are looking to have your need for a good scare satisfied. Just remember to keep an eye out for the hazy figures in the shadows. It's possible they aren't just actors trying to pull a fast one on you ... but, rather, ghosts trying to TERRIFY you.

A Ghostly Goodbye

Now that you're an expert in all things Detroit, are you ready to plan a trip of your own? Are you ready to find out for *yourself* if the Nain Rouge is real? Or if Flora Whitney really walks the grounds of the home she never knew? Are you brave enough to visit an *actually* haunted haunted house? Or face the reality that the children's voices you hear as you walk near the old Eloise Asylum might not be kids at all...but echoes from a distant, terrifying past?

If the lost souls and clever creeps of Detroit have you running for cover, we wouldn't blame you: some of Detroit's spooky specters have even us creeped out! Or maybe, after everything you've now read about Detroit, you

still don't believe in ghosts. Well, hey, that's cool. But if you're ever in Motor City and hear the sweet sound of Motown soul being played on a piano, just make sure someone is *actually playing* those wonderful melodies.

Daralynn Walker is the author of seven books for children and young adults. She is best known for her acclaimed *Madison Miles and Friends* series. Growing up in Detroit and with a librarian for a mother, Daralynn found her love for books at a young age. In school, she loved writing stories and excelled in spelling bees and writing contests. Her most recent non-fiction children's book, *Super Cities! Detroit*, explores the history of Detroit and all the fun places to visit and things to do. Daralynn resides in Atlanta, Georgia, with her husband, three lovely children, and their dog, Bailey. Visit her at www.madisonmilesandfriends.com to learn more!

Check out some of the other *Spooky America* titles available now!

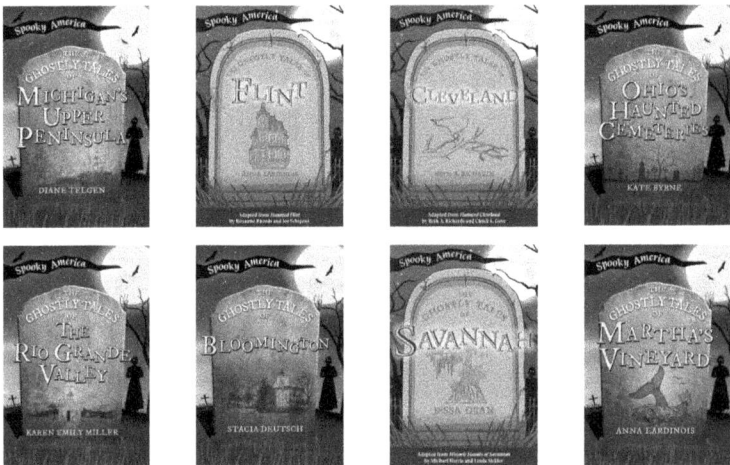

Spooky America was adapted from the creeptastic *Haunted America* series for adults. *Haunted America* explores historical haunts in cities and regions across America. Here's more from the original *Haunted Detroit* author, Nicole Beauchamp:

Visit Nicole on Instagram: @authornicolebeauchamp

www.ingramcontent.com/pod-product-compliance
Lightning Source LLC
Chambersburg PA
CBHW070347100426
42812CB00005B/1452